EX LIBRIS

....

NAME

THE ACROSTIC THEOLOGY FOR KIDS SERIES

Book 1
The Acrostic of God

·

Book 2
The Acrostic of Jesus

·

Book 3
The Acrostic of Salvation

Forthcoming 2022

·

Book 4
The Acrostic of Scripture

Forthcoming 2023

·

Book 5
The Acrostic of Bible Memory

Forthcoming 2023

A RHYMING THEOLOGY FOR KIDS

THE
ACROSTIC
OF
GOD

JONATHAN GIBSON & TIMOTHY BRINDLE

ILLUSTRATED BY
C. S. FRITZ

New Growth Press

New Growth Press, Greensboro, NC 27401
Text Copyright © 2021 by Jonathan Gibson and Timothy Brindle
Illustration Copyright © 2021 by C. S. Fritz

Cover/Interior Design and Typesetting: Trish Mahoney, themahoney.com
Cover/Interior illustrations: C. S. Fritz
Art typeset in Cinder by Fort Foundry

ISBN: 978-1-64507-184-6
Library of Congress Control Number: 2021937301

Printed in India

29 28 27 26 25 24 23 22   3 4 5 6 7

THE ACROSTIC THEOLOGY FOR KIDS SERIES

"And these words that I command you today shall be on your heart. You shall teach them diligently to your children, and shall talk of them when you sit in your house, and when you walk by the way, and when you lie down, and when you rise." Deuteronomy 6:6–7

The inspiration behind these acrostic books comes from John Calvin, the Genevan Reformer. In 1542, Calvin simplified his Catechism for the Genevan Church (1537) so that children could better understand and memorize the essential truths of the Christian Faith. It was entitled *The French ABCs*.

These acrostic books are not strictly catechetical (questions and answers), but they are written in that same tradition of instruction. As such, they are a means of planting the good seed of God's Word into the hearts of children, so that they might grow in the grace and knowledge of the Lord Jesus. We hope the new element of an acrostic poem set to rhyme may help the truths about God (theology), Jesus (Christology), salvation (soteriology), and Scripture (Biblical theology) to stick a little bit better. The books may be read in one sitting (either by parent/teacher or child) or they may be used for family devotions, taking one letter per day for families to meditate on, with some accompanying Bible verses.

We are praying that this series will be used by the Spirit to allow children and parents to grow in the knowledge of God and thus to love and trust him more. Enjoy!

Jonny Gibson and Timothy Brindle

See back of book for more information about how to use this book with children. Use the QR code to hear Timothy Brindle read aloud *The Acrostic of God* in rap style. To purchase *The Acrostic of God* music album, visit www.timothybrindleministries.com.

Dedication

For our children

Benjamin, Zachary, and Hannah
and
Natalia, Micaiah, Madelina, Evangeline, Justus, Asaph,
Timmy, and Sophia

"Remember also your Creator in the days of your youth."
Ecclesiastes 12:1a

In memory of

Leila and Johanna

Sisters in Christ beholding the face of God

"They will see his face."
Revelation 22:4a

PROLOGUE

Let's read the Acrostic of *God together*
To help you to make him *your awesome treasure*.
We'll read it, rap it, or *sing it—it's fun!*
Till Jesus comes back and his *kingdom has come*.

An acrostic poem uses the *alphabet*
To teach you about God, so you will *not forget*.
God does this in Scripture, like Psalm *One Nineteen;*
In Lamentations, he has a *fun rhyme scheme*.
So, from now on, we'll use the *first letter*
To help you remember and *learn better*.
He's the Alpha and Omega, from *A to Z;*
His beauty and his glory we were *made to see*.

Each page will have a name, *attribute, or a title*
Of God the Almighty that is *rooted in the Bible*.
He says, "In all your ways, *acknowledge me";*
Kids, you're not too young to learn *theology!*
What is theology? It's the *study of God,*
When we see who he is, we'll *love and applaud*.
Not just to know about him *more in our brains,*
But to know him as the God of *glory who reigns*.

So . . .

Let's read the Acrostic of *God together*
To help you to make him *your awesome treasure*.
We'll read it, rap it, or *sing it—it's fun!*
Till Jesus comes back and his *kingdom has come*.

ALMIGHTY

ALMIGHTY refers to our God as *Creator;*

Look up at the stars—stand in awe of your *Maker!*

He's the Sustainer of the whole *universe;*

He even came to this earth, 'cause he knew *you were cursed.*

....

Revelation 1:8 "I am the Alpha and the Omega," says the Lord God, "who is and who was and who is to come, **the Almighty**."

BLESSED

BLESSED is God, he's *overflowing in his gladness;*

But sin ruins us, *so we're groaning in our sadness.*

He knows that our sin will only *kill us and destroy;*

So he sent his Son to bless us and *fill us with his joy!*

....

1 Timothy 6:15 He who is **the blessed and only Sovereign,** the King of kings and Lord of lords.

Compassionate

COMPASSIONATE—God helps us in our *suffering;*

He comforts and forgives—he's such a *humble king.*

When he came down on Sinai, he wanted us to *know this;*

It's the first thing he said about who he is to *Moses.*

· ·

Exodus 34:6 The LORD passed before [Moses] and proclaimed, "The LORD, the LORD, a **compassionate** and gracious God, slow to anger and overflowing in covenant love and faithfulness." (AT)

DECREES

DECREES are God's plans for history, it's *his story*,

All based on the good pleasure of God for *his glory*.

He decreed that his Son would be stricken, *smitten on a tree;*

If you believe, it's because it was *written in his decree.*

. . . .

Ephesians 1:11 In him also we have received an inheritance, **since we have been predestined based on the decree** of him who works all things based on the counsel of his will. (AT)

2 Timothy 1:9 Who saved us and called us by means of a holy calling, not based on our works, **but based on his own decree** and grace, which he gave to us in Christ before times eternal. (AT)

ETERNAL

ETERNAL means that God will live forever without *end;*

He goes back just as far, way more than we can *comprehend!*

His attributes are everlasting to *everlasting,*

Including his love for us—so we are *never lacking.*

. . . .

Deuteronomy 33:27 The **eternal God** is your dwelling place, and underneath are the everlasting arms.

Faithful, Father

FAITHFUL—God will always *do what he promised;*

He cannot lie, he's *true and he's honest.*

He made a special promise called a *covenant,*

To save you from your sins, since Jesus took the *punishment.*

FATHER—God has always been the Father to *his Son.*

The Son works with his Father in all that *he has done.*

The Father sent his Son just to make you his *precious child;*

No longer enemies, by faith in Christ we're *reconciled.*

. . . .

Exodus 34:6 The LORD passed before him and proclaimed, "The LORD, the LORD, a compassionate and gracious God, slow to anger and overflowing in covenant love and **faithfulness**." (AT)

John 5:19 So Jesus said to them, "Truly, truly, I say to you, the Son can do nothing of his own accord, but only what he sees the Father doing. For whatever the Father does, that the Son does likewise."

Goodness

GOODNESS means God always does what is *kind and right;*

On sinners he even makes the sun *shine its light.*

"Taste and see that the LORD is good"; you'll *start to grasp this:*

In Christ, God's goodness satisfies our *heart with gladness.*

....

Psalm 34:8 Oh, taste and see that **the LORD is good!** Blessed is the man who takes refuge in him!

Psalm 65:4 Blessed is the one you choose and bring near, to dwell in your courts! **We shall be satisfied with the goodness of your house,** the holiness of your temple!

HOLY

HOLY—God is completely *different from us;*
He is perfectly pure and *infinitely just.*
Because he is holy, he hates and *abhors sin;*
Only faith in Christ makes us holy *before him.*

....

Isaiah 6:3 And one called to another and said: "Holy, holy, holy is the
LORD of hosts; the whole earth is full of his glory!"

Immortal

IMMORTAL means God cannot die or *ever perish;*

God is life itself—he's the *treasure* we should *cherish.*

The immortal God became a man—*Immanuel!*—

To die and rise for us, so we wouldn't *land in hell.*

....

1 Timothy 1:17 To the King of the ages, **immortal**, invisible, the only God, be honor and glory forever and ever. Amen.

Matthew 1:23 "Behold, the virgin shall conceive and bear a son, and they shall call his name **Immanuel.**"

JUSTICE

JUSTICE is how God always judges with *fairness;*

It's how he protects the orphan from the *careless.*

God never plays favorites—whether you're *rich or you're poor;*

With justice, King Jesus will return to *fix and restore.*

. . . .

Deuteronomy 32:4 "The Rock, his work is perfect, **for all his ways are justice.** A God of faithfulness and without iniquity, **just and upright is he."**

Acts 17:31 "[God] **has fixed a day on which he will judge the world in righteousness by a man whom he has appointed;** and of this he has given assurance to all by raising him from the dead."

King

KING over his creation, ruling in his *sovereignty,*

God is the potter; we are the clay of his *pottery.*

Adam lost his *dominion,*

   when he succumbed to Satan;

So Christ came to conquer him—

   his *Kingdom has begun to break in.*

. . . .

Psalm 95:3 For the LORD is a great God, and a great **King** above all gods.

Mark 1:14–15 Now after John was arrested, Jesus came into Galilee, proclaiming the gospel of God, and saying, "The time is fulfilled, **and the kingdom of God is at hand;** repent and believe in the gospel."

LOVE

LOVE is seen most in God sending his *Only Son;*

Namely, Jesus the Christ, the perfect *Holy One.*

He teaches us to be kind to each *other and not to shove;*

But to serve our sister and *brother, since God is love.*

. . . .

John 3:16 For **God so loved the world, that he gave his only Son**, that whoever believes in him should not perish but have eternal life.

1 John 4:8–9 **Anyone who does not love does not know God, because God is love.** In this the love of God was made manifest among us, that God sent his only Son into the world, so that we might live through him.

Mercy

MERCY is God not giving us what we *all deserve;*

We really should be judged, because we all *fall and swerve.*

Even though we are sinful in our *wretched lust;*

The God of mercy became man just to *rescue us.*

....

Ephesians 2:4–5 But God, being rich in mercy, because of the great love with which he loved us, even when we were dead in our trespasses, made us alive together with Christ—by grace you have been saved.

Name

NAME means this in the Bible: God's *Name is his presence;*
God's Name is who he is—it's the *same as his essence.*
He put his Name in the Temple, to be *worshiped there;*
Let us not take his Name in vain—it *deserves our care.*

....

Exodus 34:6 The LORD passed before him and proclaimed, "The LORD, the LORD, a God merciful and gracious, slow to anger, and abounding in steadfast love and faithfulness."

1 Kings 9:3 And the LORD said to him, "I have heard your prayer and your plea, which you have made before me. I have consecrated this house that you have built, **by putting my name there forever**. My eyes and my heart will be there for all time.

Deuteronomy 5:11 "'You shall not take the name of the LORD your **God in vain**, for the LORD will not hold him guiltless who takes his name in vain."

Omnificent means that God <u>made</u> *everything;*

Therefore, he can help you and me with *anything.*

Omniscient means that God <u>knows</u> *everything;*

Therefore, he can teach you and me *anything.*

Omnipresent means that God <u>fills</u> *everything;*

So he's near you and me when we face *anything.*

Omnipotent means that God <u>can do</u> *anything;*

From nothing, he created *everything!*

....

Psalm 124:8 Our help is in the name of the LORD, who made heaven and earth.

Isaiah 46:9–10 "I am God, and there is none like me, **declaring the end from the beginning** and from ancient times things not yet done, saying, '**My counsel shall stand**, and I will accomplish all my purpose.'"

Jeremiah 23:24 "Can a man hide himself in secret places so that I cannot see him? declares the LORD. **Do I not fill heaven and earth?** declares the LORD."

Job 42:2 "I know that **you can do all things**, and that no purpose of yours can be thwarted."

PATIENCE

PATIENCE is God being very slow to *anger;*

He even sent Jesus to save us from our *danger.*

When falsely accused, Jesus waited *patiently instead,*

As he trusted his Father to *raise him from the dead.*

....

Jonah 4:2b For I knew that you are a gracious God and merciful, **slow to anger** and abounding in steadfast love, and relenting from disaster.

1 Peter 2:23 When he was reviled, he did not revile in return; when he suffered, he did not threaten, **but continued entrusting himself to him who judges justly.**

QUICK

QUICK—God is faster than shooting stars *seen at night;*

His Word works even faster than the *speed of light.*

Jesus Christ spoke to raise the dead—like with *Lazarus;*

He's quick to forgive, even those who are *blasphemous.*

....

Nehemiah 9:17b "But you are a God **ready to forgive**, gracious and merciful, slow to anger and abounding in steadfast love."

John 11:43–44 When he had said these things, he cried out with a loud voice, **"Lazarus, come out."** The man who had died came out, his hands and feet bound with linen strips, and his face wrapped with a cloth. Jesus said to them, "Unbind him, and let him go."

Righteousness

RIGHTEOUSNESS is God's absolute *standard of pure perfection;*

Jesus obeyed all the *commandments for your sure redemption.*

He gives his righteousness by faith as the *greatest present;*

He'll help you obey and see his righteous *ways are pleasant.*

. . . .

Romans 3:21–22 But now the righteousness of God has been manifested apart from the law, although the Law and the Prophets bear witness to it—the righteousness of God through faith in Jesus Christ for all who believe.

אנכי

לא

לא

תרצה

תנאף

לא תגנב

...ור לא תענה

תחמד

כבד

Simplicity

SIMPLICITY means that God is One; think *upon this:*

God really only has one attribute—his *God-ness.*

Therefore, no one can see his face and *remain alive;*

Since his glory is so great, there's no way *we'd survive.*

I know his simplicity might be *hard to discuss,*

But God is One—therefore he has no *parts, unlike us.*

Every single thing about him is *all divine,*

For God is everything that he is—*all the time.*

....

Deuteronomy 6:4 "Hear, O Israel: The LORD our God, **the LORD is one.**"

Exodus 33:20 "But," he said, "you cannot see my face, **for man shall not see me and live.**"

TRINITY

TRINITY—this word should make you praise when you *hear it;*

It means God is the Father, Son, and Holy *Spirit.*

One God in three persons, though we *can't comprehend it;*

It comes from Scripture—it's nothing *man has invented.*

The Father, Son, and Spirit deserve the *same praises;*

The Bible teaches that they each share the *same greatness!*

The Father sent his Son who came down just to *save us,*

Then gave his Spirit—the Trinity is so *gracious!*

....

Matthew 28:19 Go therefore and make disciples of all nations, baptizing them **in the name of the Father and of the Son and of the Holy Spirit.**

Acts 2:33 Being therefore exalted at the right hand of God, and having received from the Father the promise of the Holy Spirit, [Jesus] has poured out this that you yourselves are seeing and hearing.

Unchangeable

UNCHANGEABLE—God cannot change in his *substance;*

He's perfect already, no need for *adjustments.*

He can't get any greater—he's not *improvable;*

Another way to say this: he's *immutable.*

....

Malachi 3:6 For I the Lord **do not change**; therefore you, O children of Jacob, are not consumed.

James 1:17 Every good gift and every perfect gift is from above, coming down from **the Father of lights, with whom there is no variation or shadow due to change.**

Veracious

VERACIOUS means that God always *speaks the truth;*

From his Son's resurrection, we can *see the proof.*

We can tell God's Word has perfect *veracity;*

He foretells what'll happen with *tenacity.*

....

Psalm 119:160 The sum of your word is truth, and every one of your righteous rules endures forever.

WRATH

WRATH is God's anger towards the sin of *Satan and people;*

Because he loves what is right, he has *hatred of evil.*

So, if God did not have wrath,

  then he would be *pleased with sin;*

But he poured out his wrath on Christ

  for those who *believe in him.*

....

Nahum 1:2–3 The LORD is a jealous and avenging God; **the LORD is avenging and wrathful**; the LORD takes vengeance on his adversaries and keeps wrath for his enemies. **The LORD is slow to anger and great in power, and the LORD will by no means clear the guilty.**

EXCELLENT

EXCELLENT—God is full of *majesty and splendor;*

The love he has for you and *has for me is tender.*

His perfection is the most *precious thing—truly;*

Our one request is to see his *excellence and beauty!*

....

Psalm 29:2 Ascribe to the LORD the glory due his name; worship the LORD in the **beauty of holiness**. (AT)

Psalm 27:4 One thing have I asked of the LORD, that will I seek after: that I may dwell in the house of the LORD all the days of my life, **to gaze upon the beauty of the LORD** and to inquire in his temple.

YESHUA

YESHUA is the word for "Jesus" in *Hebrew;*

It means "salvation"—he can forgive and *free you.*

When the Old Testament says, "Yahweh is my *Yeshua,"*

It's a clue that on the cross Jesus was our *Joshua.*

....

Isaiah 12:2 "Behold, **God is my salvation**; I will trust, and will not be afraid; for the LORD GOD is my strength and my song, and **he has become my salvation.**"

Matthew 1:21 "She will bear a son, **and you shall call his name Jesus, for he will save his people from their sins.**"

ZEAL

ZEAL refers to God's powerful *determination*,

To show his glory in the history of *salvation*.

Jesus was zealous for God's glory—died to *vindicate it;*

His Spirit fills us with his zeal—now our *sin, we hate it!*

....

Isaiah 9:6–7 For to us a child is born, to us a son is given; and the government shall be upon his shoulder, and his name shall be called Wonderful Counselor, Mighty God, Everlasting Father, Prince of Peace. Of the increase of his government and of peace there will be no end, on the throne of David and over his kingdom, to establish it and to uphold it with justice and with righteousness from this time forth and forevermore. **The zeal of the LORD of hosts will do this.**

Closing Refrain

Now we've read the Acrostic of God *together*,

Ask God to be the One whom you want and *treasure*.

Thank him for who he is and *what he has done;*

"Father in heaven, help me to *trust in your Son."*

RHYME YOUR ACROSTIC

Since the beginning of time, human beings have been using acrostics and rhyme as a teaching tool. Putting ideas into an acrostic rhyme helps children to learn things in a more memorable way than simple rote learning. God, the author of all language, knows this. The Bible is full of poetry. It contains acrostic poems that begin lines with each letter of the Hebrew alphabet (e.g., Psalm 119 and the book of Lamentations); it also contains poems that emphasize rhyme in Hebrew (e.g., Psalms 1 and 2). These poetic features make the content of God's Word easier to remember. Acrostic poems are straightforward, covering each letter of the alphabet, A–Z. The Acrostic Theology for Kids series is written as a rap. Children might be more familiar with this style of rhyme than their parents. If you need some help reading it, there is a QR code at the end of the book that you can scan to hear Timothy Brindle read *The Acrostic of God* in a rap style.

Basic Truths to Memorize with Children

THE LORD'S PRAYER

OUR FATHER in heaven,
hallowed be your name,
your kingdom come,
your will be done,
on earth as it is in heaven.
Give us this day our daily bread;
And forgive us our debts,
as we forgive our debtors.
And lead us not into temptation
but deliver us from evil.
For yours is the kingdom, and the power,
and the glory, forever. Amen.

THE TEN COMMANDMENTS

AND GOD spoke all these words, saying, I am the LORD your God, who brought you out of the land of Egypt, out of the house of slavery.

1. You shall have no other gods before me.

2. You shall not make for yourself a carved image, or any likeness of anything that is in heaven above, or that is in the earth beneath, or that is in the water under the earth.

3. You shall not take the name of the LORD your God in vain, for the LORD will not hold him guiltless who takes his name in vain.

4. Remember the Sabbath day, to keep it holy. Six days you shall labor, and do all your work, but the seventh day is a Sabbath to the LORD your God.

5. Honor your father and your mother, that your days may be long in the land that the LORD your God is giving you.

6. You shall not murder.

7. You shall not commit adultery.

8. You shall not steal.

9. You shall not bear false witness against your neighbor.

10. You shall not covet your neighbor's house; you shall not covet your neighbor's wife, or his male servant, or his female servant, or his ox, or his donkey, or anything that is your neighbor's.

THE APOSTLES' CREED

I BELIEVE in God, the Father Almighty,
    Maker of heaven and earth.

I believe in Jesus Christ, his only-begotten Son, our Lord;
    who was conceived by the Holy Spirit,
    born of the Virgin Mary;
    suffered under Pontius Pilate;
    was crucified, dead, and buried;
    he descended into hell;
    the third day he rose again from the dead;
    he ascended into heaven,
    and sits at the right hand of God the Father Almighty;
    from there he shall come to judge the living and the dead.

I believe in the Holy Spirit;
    the holy catholic Church;
    the communion of saints;
    the forgiveness of sins;
    the resurrection of the body;
    and the life everlasting. Amen.

 Scan this QR code to hear Timothy Brindle read *The Acrostic of God* in a rap style. To purchase *The Acrostic of God* music album, visit www.timothybrindleministries.com.